Ro

Jon

Illustrated by
Jane Bottomley

One day, Josh went to the pet shop.
"Have you got any dogs?" he
asked.

"No dogs," said Mrs Tickle. "Only Rover."

Mrs Tickle took Josh to the back room. In a box was a spider. It was as big as a dog.

Rover looked up with his big sad eyes. Eight big sad eyes.

"OK," said Josh, "I'll have him."

Josh took Rover home. He trained him to beg.

He trained him to fetch a stick...

...to roll over for a tickle...

...and to sleep on the end of his bed.

In the Morning

Three big boys grabbed Josh.
"We want your lunch!" they said.

Josh called for Rover. Rover raced around the corner.

It's a monster!

The big boys didn't stay long.

Next Day

Rover was hungry.

When Josh woke up, Rover was gone.

Josh looked for Rover. He saw the three big boys.
"Help!" they said. "A bug!"

A monster bug!

AAAAAAAA!

Josh saw the bug. It was as big as a cat!

Josh and the boys raced around the corner. Then they got a shock.
"A web," said Josh.

The web was enormous! It was Rover's web.

SPLAT

The bug went smack into the web. Rover had trapped it!

"You have a great pet!" said the big boys. Josh hugged Rover.

Rover rolled over for a tickle.